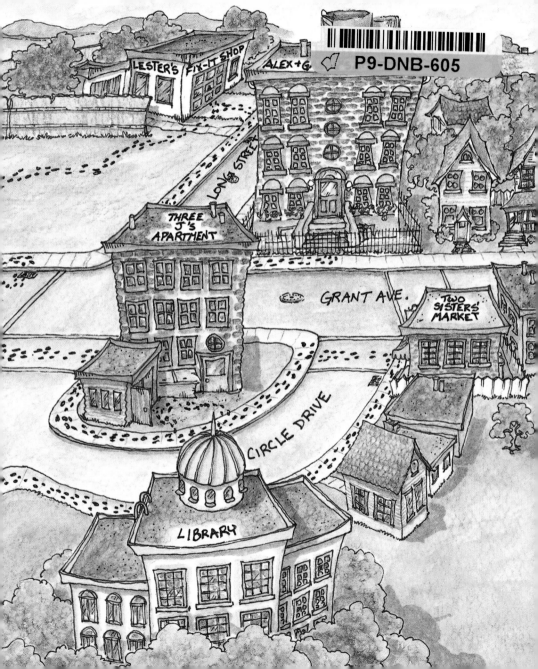

Rookie choices™

A FLAG FOR ALL

Written by Larry Dane Brimner • Illustrated by Christine Tripp

Children's Press®
A Division of Scholastic Inc.
New York • Toronto • London • Auckland • Sydney
Mexico City • New Delhi • Hong Kong
Danbury, Connecticut

For the Cajon Valley schools, where it all began
—L.D.B.

For my father
—C.T.

Reading Consultants
Linda Cornwell
Literacy Specialist

Katharine A. Kane
Education Consultant
(Retired, San Diego County Office of Education and San Diego State University)

Library of Congress Cataloging-in-Publication Data

Brimner, Larry Dane.
  A flag for all / written by Larry Dane Brimner ; illustrated by Christine Tripp.
      p. cm.— (Rookie choices)
Summary: While researching the American flag for a class project, the Corner Kids ask townspeople what the flag means to them and find that each person has a different answer.
  ISBN 0-516-22544-8 (lib. bdg.) 0-516-27792-8 (pbk.)
  [1. Flags—United States—Fiction. 2. Flag Day—Fiction. 3.Holidays—Fiction. 4. Patriotism—Fiction.] I. Tripp, Christine, ill. II. Title. III. Series.
  PZ7.B767 Fl 2002
  [Fic] —dc21
                        2002001613

CHILDREN'S PRESS, AND ROOKIE CHOICES™, and associated logos are trademarks and or registered trademarks of Grolier Publishing Co., Inc. SCHOLASTIC and associated logos are trademarks and or registered trademarks of Scholastic Inc.
1 2 3 4 5 6 7 8 9 10 R 11 10 09 08 07 06 05 04 03 02

This book is about **patriotism**.

The Corner Kids were at the library finding out about the American flag. Mr. Toddle wanted his class to come up with a Flag Day celebration that would show all the things the flag means.

"The flag means a lot of things," Gabby said to Three J and Alex. The three friends called themselves the Corner Kids because they lived on corners of the same street.

7

"There's a star for each state," said Three J.

Gabby nodded. "And the stripes are for the thirteen colonies that first made up America," she said.

Alex sighed. "Listen to this," he said. "'The flag means different things to different people.'"

"How will we find out what it means to *everybody*?" asked Three J.

"We'll ask," said Gabby.

Three J's eyes opened wide. "Everybody?" he asked.

Gabby laughed. "No, silly. Just follow me."

She went to the check-out counter. "What does our flag mean to you?" Gabby asked the librarian.

15

The librarian told them that the flag stands for America, and America means freedom. "I can read any book I want," she said.

At Two Sisters' Market the short sister said the flag means she helps choose the leaders. "I vote in every election," she said.

19

Mr. Yang, the doorman at Three J's building, told them the flag means hope. "The flag tells me that if I work hard, I can have a good life in this country."

21

The next day at school, everybody shared. Then Mr. Toddle asked, "How do we celebrate something that means so many things?"

Nobody had any ideas.

Then Gabby noticed something. Three J was wearing a red shirt. Alex had on a blue shirt. Her own shirt was white. She began to get an idea.

"Let's make a people flag on the playground," she said. "Everyone in town can help. That will show that the flag is about people and all the different ways they love America."

On Flag Day the whole town formed a flag.

It was a flag for all.

ABOUT THE AUTHOR

Larry Dane Brimner studied literature and writing at San Diego State University and taught school for twenty years. The author of more than seventy-five books for children, many of them Children's Press titles, he enjoys meeting young readers and writers when he isn't at his computer.

ABOUT THE ILLUSTRATOR

Christine Tripp lives in Ottawa, Canada, with her husband Don; four grown children—Elizabeth, Erin, Emily, and Eric; son-in-law Jason; grandsons Brandon and Kobe; four cats; and one very large, scruffy puppy named Jake.